LOREE GRIFFIN BURNS

Photographs by **ELLEN HARASIMOWICZ**

Beetle Busters

A Rogue Insect and the People Who Track It

Houghton Mifflin Harcourt

Boston   New York

For Ed Schroth, Clint McFarland, Bruce Palmer, and Ryan Zumpano, four men I admire —L.G.B.

For my boys, Jeff, Craig, and Reed —E.H.

Book design by YAY! Design
Tree and forest illustrations by Rachel Newborn
The text was set in Weidemann.

All images by Ellen Harasimowicz with the exception of those on the following pages: 8: U.S. Forest Service, Northeastern
Area, State and Private Forestry // 18, left: Dennis Haugen, USDA Forest Service // 18, bottom right: Stephen Lavallee,
Courtesy USDA/APHIS // 19, 26: Courtesy USDA/APHIS // 22–23: Mike Bohne/U.S. Forest Service // 24: University of
Vermont, Entomology Research Laboratory // 35–36, 38–39: Kevin Dodds/U.S. Forest Service // 44: © 2011 Canadian Science
Publishing. Reproduced with permission from Dodds and Orwig. *Canadian Journal of Forest Research* 41: 1–14. // 58: Loree
Griffin Burns

The Library of Congress has cataloged the hardcover edition as follows:
Burns, Loree Griffin. Beetle busters : a rogue insect and the people who track it / Loree Griffin Burns ; photographs by
Ellen Harasimowicz. pages cm. (Scientists in the field) Audience: Ages 1–14. Audience: Grade 7 to 8. 1. Asian longhorned
beetle—Juvenile literature. 2. Beetles—Juvenile literature. I. Harasimowicz, Ellen, photographer. II. Title. SB945.A83B87 2014
595.76'48dc23 2013050160

ISBN: 978-0-547-79267-5 hardcover
ISBN: 978-1-328-89572-1 paperback

Manufactured in China
SCP 10 9 8 7 6 5 4 3 2 1
4500703568

CONTENTS

The Cut

Ryan Zumpano has seen a lot of neat things in the woods: turtles, snakes, woodpeckers as big as cats. Among the neatest, though, was a certain pair of common white-tailed deer. He and a friend were walking in the woods near an old landfill in their hometown, exploring. The two boys and the two deer were within six feet of one another before either pair realized the others were there. All four animals stopped.

The boys stared.

The deer moved their noses, searching for a scent.

At some mysterious signal—the boys didn't see or hear it—the deer exploded into action. The larger one made a massive leap for the woods, covering a distance of twelve feet or more in a single leap. And as it did, it made a spectacular noise: a sharp, rushing vocalization probably meant to scare the boys.

"It was the loudest, coolest noise I've ever heard," Ryan says.

When you spend time in the woods, these sorts of experiences just happen. That's why Ryan spends so much time there.

He remembers his worst day in these woods just as vividly. It happened years ago, but he's still not over it. He was hanging out with another friend near the same spot where he'd seen the deer.

"We came down after school," Ryan remembers. "We walked the same route we always do, a path through thick woods. There were trees on both sides of us, as usual. But at a certain place, they stopped. *The trees stopped*. They were gone."

The boys stood in the woods that they knew better than anyone else around and tried to understand what they were seeing. Who would cut down their trees?

"We had no idea what to do. We took pictures with our phones. We tried to figure out what was happening."

The boys eventually found a sign posted at the place where the woods used to meet a main road into the center of town. The sign explained that part of the forest was being cut because of a beetle. They took more pictures and sent all of them to their science teacher. Mr. Palmer ran the Biodiversity Club at Ryan's school, and he'd grown up exploring these same woods. He'd taught Ryan and the other members of the club everything they knew about birding, tracking animals, identifying trees, and working in the woods as naturalists. In fact, it was Mr. Palmer who had introduced Ryan to this particular patch of forest.

"My first reaction," Mr. Palmer remembers, "was the same as Ryan's: heartbreak."

Although Mr. Palmer understood what Ryan was feeling, not many others did. Sure, people felt bad that Ryan was so upset, but they didn't really feel for the trees.

"They'd say, 'Sorry to hear your favorite place is ruined,'" Ryan remembers. "But they didn't understand. That forest was like our home. And in two days, it was gone."

After thinking about it a while longer, Ryan repeats something he has said often about the cut at the landfill: "I still don't know what to do."

But in reality, Ryan *has* been doing something. Since the cut, he and Mr. Palmer and the rest of their middle/high school Biodiversity Club have continued to do just what they've always done on the property around the old landfill: monitor wildlife. They've continued to count birds and record animal tracks, and they've added their recent findings to the eleven years of records that Biodiversity Club members had collected before the cut.

"As much as I hate what happened here," says Mr. Palmer, "as a teacher, I see opportunity."

What kind of opportunity?

Well, right now, in the woods of central Massachusetts, humankind is taking an unprecedented stand against an invasive beetle. As a result, these woods hold an opportunity to learn about the beetle, the forest it threatens, and the interaction between the two. And in the coming years, there will be an opportunity to answer the one question that has weighed on Ryan Zumpano's mind for the past two years:

Was cutting those trees the right thing to do?

The Beetle

People who work with Asian longhorned beetles can't help themselves. They spend a lot of their time looking at trees.

"It's an interesting way to see a city," Clint McFarland says, "going block to block and looking at the trees. Sometimes people in places like New York City joke, 'Do we have any trees?' But they *are* there, all around you."

Clint McFarland, federal project manager for the Asian Longhorned Beetle Cooperative Eradication Program in Massachusetts, scanning a tree for beetles.

And it's true: no matter where you live—big city or small town—chances are, there are trees around you. They may be few and far between in the city, or in certain climates, but they're there. And no matter where they are, trees are doing important things. They beautify the landscape, create shade, freshen the air, reduce noise, filter groundwater, anchor soil, give shelter to animals, and sometimes even shelter people. Trees make our lives on earth better—can you even imagine our world without them?—but they do it so quietly and with so little fanfare that most of the time we forget they're doing it at all. Until they're not.

Which is exactly why Clint walks around cities looking up into trees. He's searching for an insect that preys on them. The Asian longhorned beetle is a pest with powerful jaws and a taste for wood, a beetle that evolved on the other side of the planet and that has recently found itself here, in the trees of North American cities. Clint and his colleagues believe that unless these beetles are stopped, they will move out of the city and into the surrounding forests, damaging and killing trees as they go.

"What do we have to lose?" Clint asks. He takes a deep breath and exhales before answering his own question: "The entire northeastern hardwood forest."

Eastern Hardwood Forests

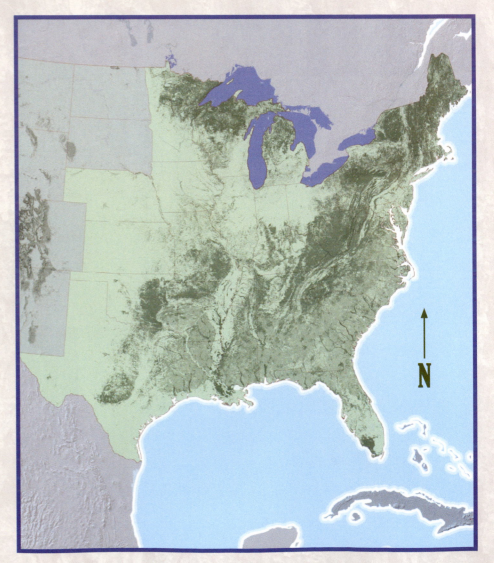

The dark green areas on this map represent a huge swath of heavily treed land in the eastern United States.

An adult Asian longhorned beetle.

The Asian longhorned beetle (ALB for short) is a stunner. Its 1.5-inch body is deep black speckled with white, and its head bears a set of shockingly long striped antennae. These antennae and the beetle's six feet are tinted blue, and its mouthparts, if you get close enough to see them, resemble a miniature lobster claw. If an Asian longhorned beetle landed next to you right now, you would probably never forget it. Somehow, though, these flashy insects are hard to spot in the wild.

"You'd be surprised," Clint says, "how camouflaged that coloration is up in a tree. Even after you spot one, see the antennae moving, or notice the stripes, it's easy to lose sight of the beetle when you take the binoculars down."

Tricky camouflage is just one of the reasons the beetles are so hard to find in the forest. They also spend most of their lives—up to two years in some cases—*inside* trees.

This clandestine life cycle begins in late summer when a female selects a tree on which to mate and lay her eggs. She

eggs

early larva

chooses carefully, searching out one of the dozen or more types of tree on which her young can thrive. For the record, this includes many of the major North American forest trees: maples, birches, elms, poplars, willows, and ash, to name just a few.

Once she's found a suitable tree, a pregnant female uses her powerful jaws to chew a pit into its bark. When she reaches the soft tissue just underneath, she deposits a single egg into the pit. (Scientists call this an oviposition pit.) Then she walks away. In about two weeks, a legless grub, barely visible to the human eye, emerges from the egg. Although the larva looks nothing like an adult beetle yet, its mouthparts are almost as strong. It uses them to chew farther into the softest part of the tree, cutting through crucial tissues as it does.

When a larva is strong enough, it moves even deeper into the tree, gouging tunnels and leaving sawdust frass, or excrement, in its wake. By the time the first frosts of winter arrive, the larva has settled deep in the heartwood of its host tree, safe from predators and protected from the elements. It will spend the winter this way. Except for the oviposition pit, which is very hard to see, you might never even know the beetle was in there.

When spring arrives, the larva begins to feed and grow again. How quickly it reaches maturity now depends on two things: how far the larva had developed before the winter set in, and the climate around the tree. For Asian longhorned beetles, maturity means becoming a giant grub as long and as thick as an adult human's thumb. In warmer climates a larva

late larva

The various stages of the Asian longhorned beetle life cycle. These pictures were taken in a laboratory where the beetles are raised in captivity. While eggs can sometimes be seen in the wild, the larval and pupal life stages normally happen out of sight—that is, inside a tree.

pupa

will reach maturity about eleven months after hatching from an egg. In cooler climates, the larva can take longer to mature, so it needs a second winter inside the tree. Eventually, though, each larva will pupate, transforming from a grub into a full-sized adult beetle right inside the tree. The adult beetle will eventually chew its way out of the tree in order to begin the cycle all over again, leaving in its wake one more frass-filled tunnel. This last tunnel ends with a perfectly round exit hole in the bark of the tree.

    A single ALB larva cannot kill a tree. It damages a tree by tunneling through its trunk or branches, weakening the tree structurally and hampering its ability to feed itself at the same time. But since a single female beetle can lay more than twenty-five eggs in her lifetime, and since her instinct is to lay these eggs on the same tree, most infested trees don't house a single larva. Most are home to an entire family of beetles. Given enough time, this hungry family *can* kill a tree—or at least weaken it to the point of collapse. Given even more time, the family could grow large enough to cause this sort of damage to an entire forest.

An adult Asian longhorned beetle next to the exit hole it chewed on the way out of its host tree. The exit hole is smaller than a dime.

Knowing the details of the Asian longhorned beetle life cycle helps Clint track it down, despite its elusive coloration and hidden development. During the late summer months, he and his team can use binoculars to looks for adult beetles on the outside of trees. But they can look for signs that the beetles might be lurking inside a tree—the telltale scratch of an egg-laying site, the dripping sap or accumulating sawdust that sometimes marks these sites, or perfectly round beetle exit holes—all year round.

What do they do when they find these signs? That's where the story gets complicated. The only way to kill Asian longhorned beetles and larvae living inside a tree is to cut down the tree and chip it to pieces. And the only way to stop adult beetles living outside of trees from finding and infesting new ones is to cut down and chip potential host trees, whether or not there are beetles in them. To many people, this is an awful conundrum: to save trees, we have to kill the beetle, but to eliminate the beetle, we have to kill a lot of trees.

So, what do you think?

If cutting trees in one community today would save the trees in *your* backyard tomorrow, is it worth it?

Would you feel the same way if you lived in that community, and the trees being cut down were the only ones in your entire neighborhood?

Can you find the four ALB egg-laying sites on the bark of this tree? It's tricky. And it gets trickier when you realize that how egg-laying sites look varies with the age of the site and the type of tree it's scratched into. (See, for example, the images on page 18.)

A Life in Rings

Lots of things affect the growth of a tree. These include how much sunlight, rain, and nutrients the tree receives, as well as the climate conditions, diseases, and natural disasters it encounters during its life. You can usually get a sense for how a tree is doing simply by watching it. But if you could look inside a tree, you'd get a detailed picture of not only how well the tree is doing at that moment, but how well it has grown during every single year of its life. This is possible because there is a pattern to how a tree grows, and that pattern is captured in the wood of the tree's trunk and branches.

The science of examining the growth rings of trees and matching them to specific years in time is called dendrochronology. It starts with a cookie. Not the kind you eat, of course, but the kind you get when you cut a cross-section from a tree trunk. (It's called a cookie because once cut, the round cross-section of trunk resembles an oversized cookie.)

At the outer edge of each tree cookie is the bark. This protective layer can be thick or thin, smooth or patterned,

13

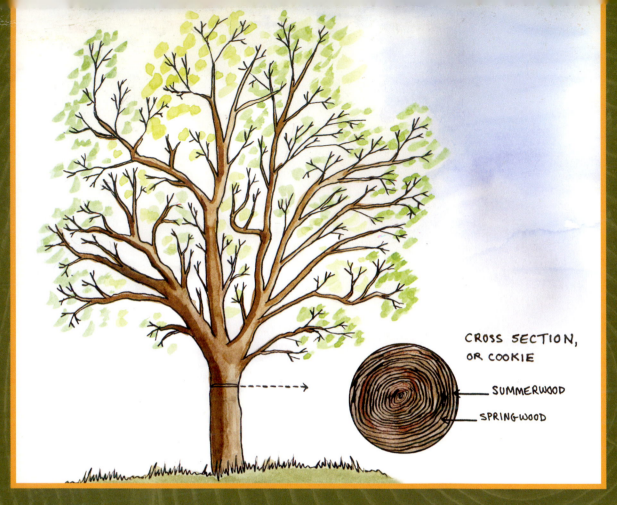

CROSS SECTION, OR COOKIE

SUMMERWOOD

SPRINGWOOD

dye. Dendrochronologists can then visualize each year of tree growth as a wide band of lightly colored springwood coupled to a thinner, darker band of summerwood. (In places like Massachusetts, trees don't grow at all in the fall and winter.) Together these bands are known as growth rings.

The relative width of the growth rings throughout the cookie says something about the growing conditions during the year in question: the wider the band, the better the growth. When conditions are poor—during a drought, for example—the tree doesn't grow much. Its growth rings are likely to be narrow. When conditions are perfect—lots of sun and rain and no natural disasters—the growth rings can be very wide. By comparing the growth rings of trees growing in a single geographic area, dendrochronologists can piece together the natural and climate history of a place.

When scientists want to examine the growth history of a tree without cutting it down, they remove core samples from the tree. Using a special drill (called an increment borer), a thin piece of wood that stretches from the bark to the center of the tree is removed. The cores can often be sanded and stained in the same way as a tree cookie, allowing scientists to study the individual years in a tree's history without sacrificing the tree itself.

depending on the type of tree and its age. Bark serves the tree much like your skin serves you: it insulates the tree and keeps bad things—insects, fungi, and bacteria, for example—out of it. Beneath the bark are layers of tissue that are responsible for moving nutrients and water from leaves down to the trunk and roots, and from the roots up to the branches and leaves. In between these two layers is a third layer, called the vascular cambium. The cambium layer is responsible for producing the cells that become the tree's wood.

In springtime, when the growth season begins (at least in the northeastern United States), the cambium layer produces large cells with very thin walls. These cells form wood that is light in color. Later in the summer, as the tree's growth slows down, the cambium layer produces smaller cells with thicker walls. These cells form wood that is darker in color. The color difference between wood produced in the spring (called springwood) and wood produced in the summer (called summerwood) can be made even more visible by exposing tree cookies to

CHAPTER TWO

Fall in New England.

The Trees

The story of the Asian longhorned beetle in North America begins in northern China, where the insect was once a harmless part of the environment. In the 1970s, however, the Chinese government decided to replant a forest that had been whittled away over time. Instead of modeling the new forest on the old one and patiently planting a variety of trees that were common to northern China, officials chose to plant faster-growing trees, including a type of poplar from North America. Tens of thousands of these poplars were planted, and as they began to mature, project leaders made an awful discovery: poplar is an outstanding host for ALB. They thrive in it. And so the beetle flourished in this strange new forest. Within a decade, the ALB population in China had exploded. Officials decided to cut down the dying trees and start replanting the forest properly.

But what would they do with all those downed poplar trees? The safest thing would have been to chip all the wood, ensuring that any beetles or beetle larvae inside were killed. Instead, the wood was used to make things. Some of the things they produced were wooden pallets, spools, and shipping crates that could be used to load goods on and off cargo ships. As soon as these pallets and spools and crates arrived in Chinese port cities, they were loaded with goods and shipped overseas.

16

Here, hundreds of wooden shipping pallets are stacked outside a business. When in use, individual pallets are loaded with items to be shipped and a forklift is used to transport the load, on its pallet, from one location to another.

Have you guessed what was lurking in the wood of those shipping pallets, spools, and crates?

Asian longhorned beetle larvae.

Lots of them.

Amazingly, larval development continued inside the cut wood. Instead of maturing and burrowing their way out of standing poplar trees, adult beetles that survived the tree chopping and crate building simply matured and burrowed their way out of wooden shipping crates. In a surprising number of cases, beetles emerged after shipping. They were now thousands of miles from their homeland.

"It's a miracle that Asian longhorned beetle infestations take hold at all," says Mike Bohne, a U.S. Forest Service scientist who has studied ALB for years. "You have to have a female get out and find a host tree, and then a male to also find that host tree. It's amazing that it ever happens."

And yet, somehow, it has happened. Six times.

The first time was in New York City. In 1996, a man named Ingram Carner noticed strange holes in maple trees near his Brooklyn property. Mr. Carner was convinced that neighborhood troublemakers were responsible, and he set out to catch them in the act. He parked in a lot near the trees and waited for the vandals to show up. While waiting, he studied the trees. That's how Mr. Carner managed to witness a large black and white beetle chew its way out of a tree. The maples weren't being drilled by hoodlums—they were being eaten by beetles.

It didn't take long for officials in New York to identify the beetles Mr. Carner found as the foreign Asian longhorned beetle, or to surmise that they'd arrived via shipping products in New York's nearby harbor. Given the scarcity of trees in the city, however, they felt it was unlikely the beetles had spread very far. In fact, they thought it might be possible to carefully

The most common signs of ALB damage are egg-laying sites and exit holes (left photo), and these are sometimes highlighted by dripping sap (not pictured) and frass (top right). When they are ready to exit a tree, adult ALBs don't let anything get in their way, not even tin tree tags (bottom right).

18

search trees in the area, identify those harboring beetles, and cut them all down. A city forest, after all, is very different from a wild one. In the city, particularly a large one such as New York, trees are pretty isolated. A dozen of them may line the two sides of a street, for example, creating a beautiful, shade-providing canopy. But these trees are like a leafy green island growing in a sea of concrete. As far as the beetles living on this island know, these dozen trees are the only ones available. And if the beetles living on this island happen to be awkward fliers, as Asian longhorned beetles are, they might be inclined to live on the small island for a very long time. Long enough to be captured and destroyed.

ALB Infestations in North America

In 1996, North America's first Asian longhorned beetle eradication program was launched in New York City. Government workers began by inspecting every single potential host tree within a certain distance of the infested trees in Brooklyn. When signs of ALB were found in a tree, it was cut down and chipped into pieces.

Two years into the project, another Asian longhorned beetle infestation was discovered, this time in Chicago, Illinois.

Two years after that, another was found in Jersey City, New Jersey. In 2003, ALB was discovered in Toronto, Canada.

In each city, beetles were thought to have arrived at nearby ports in wooden shipping products. In each city, officials set up an eradication program modeled after the one in New York. At the same time, an international law requiring all wooden shipping products to be chemically treated in order to kill ALB (and any other insects that might be lurking in the wood) was passed. The law was designed to keep new infestations out of the country. But there was no way to know how many infestations were already *in* the country.

An aerial view of an urban forest in Worcester, Massachusetts.

In August 2008, Mike Bohne got a phone call from Massachusetts. A woman in the city of Worcester (WUSS-ter) had found several black and white beetles with long striped antennae crawling on the trees in her yard. She thought they might be Asian longhorned beetles.

"I'd been called hundreds of times throughout my career by people thinking they had seen an Asian longhorned beetle," Mike remembers, "and every single time, it wasn't ALB. I went down to Worcester not really knowing what I'd see." Worcester is the second-largest city in Massachusetts, but it's much smaller than New York City or Chicago or the other cities working to eradicate ALB. Worcester is only an hour's drive from the borders of Vermont, New Hampshire, and Maine, three very heavily treed states. And instead of being surrounded by other cities and city forests, Worcester is surrounded by rural towns—and wild, natural forests.

In a natural forest, many tree species grow in close proximity to one another. They compete for sunlight from above and nutrients from below, and their crowns—the leafy tops—often touch. A beetle living in a natural, wild forest can move between trees without flying at all, walking from the canopy of one tree into the canopy of the tree growing next to it. Unlike in a city forest, this canopy stretches on and on and on. In the northeastern part of the United States, in fact, it stretches all the way into Canada. In a natural forest like the one outside of Worcester, Massachusetts, it would be difficult, maybe impossible, to find and destroy every last Asian longhorned beetle.

21

By the time Mike arrived in Worcester, his colleagues had verified the worst: the beetles observed by the homeowner were indeed ALB.

"The weather was really bad when we arrived—it was torrential rain—so our initial survey of trees was limited," Mike remembers. He and the other scientists examined dozens of trees and found signs of an ALB

Clint McFarland in Worcester.

infestation, but nothing too worrisome. "Originally, there was a thought that maybe the infestation wasn't that bad."

But then Mike visited an industrial area on the northern edge of the city, not far from where the original insects had been found. A seventy-foot, eighty-year-old maple standing across the street from a manufacturing plant caught his eye.

"I noticed the tree was already starting to show fall coloration," he says. "It was only August, though, so I suspected it might be infested. I parked my car and walked toward it. It had a very healthy-looking crown."

As Mike got closer, however, he could see the tree was far from healthy: its entire trunk and most of the main branches were riddled with ALB exit holes.

"The beetles had attacked this tree literally everywhere. It was the most heavily infested tree I'd ever seen."

And that's not all. Mike began to see live beetles in this part of the city, and they were frightening. "The beetles were enormous," he recalls. "They were the largest Asian longhorned beetles I had ever seen; I never saw beetles that big

22

From a distance, the only clue that something was amiss with this seventy-foot maple was the early seasonal color high in its canopy.

Closer up, Mike Bohne found the maple's trunk and branches riddled with ALB exit holes. This tree is now believed to have been Worcester's "mother tree," the first ALB host tree in the city. It was cut and chipped in 2008.

in New York or Chicago or in China."

Over the next few days, Mike and his colleagues began to grasp the seriousness of the situation in Worcester. All signs seemed to indicate that ALB had been living and reproducing in and around the industrial part of the city for years—perhaps as many as fifteen or twenty. City trees were heavily infested, and the question on everyone's mind was this: Could the beetles have moved out of the city and into the natural forest around Worcester? If so, eradication in Worcester was going to involve chasing ALB into a natural forest. No one was sure if this could be done, especially when the beetle had such a head start.

Even Clint McFarland, who had worked on the New York infestation for years and was called in to lead the eradication effort in Worcester, worried when he got there and saw for himself the city's connection to the surrounding forest.

Says Clint, "I never had nightmares about trees until I came to Worcester, from the point of view of what we have to lose."

Tree ID

There are nearly a thousand tree species in North America, and identifying any one of them starts with a careful look at its shape. Some groups of trees are cone-shaped (these are the evergreen trees known as conifers) and some are sphere-shaped (these are the deciduous trees called broadleaf trees).

You can further identify trees by closely examining their leaves or, in the case of conifers, their needles. The contour of leaves (Are they smooth or toothed along the edge? Are they lobed?) and needles (Are their edges round or square?), as well as how they are arranged on branches, provides clues to a tree's identity. The color, texture, and pattern of a tree's bark are also useful details, as are the type, size, and shape of each tree's fruits and seeds.

In North America, more than twelve types of trees are known to host Asian longhorned beetles in the wild, including maple, horse chestnut, willow, elm, birch, sycamore, mimosa, katsura, hackberry, ash, poplar, and mountain ash.

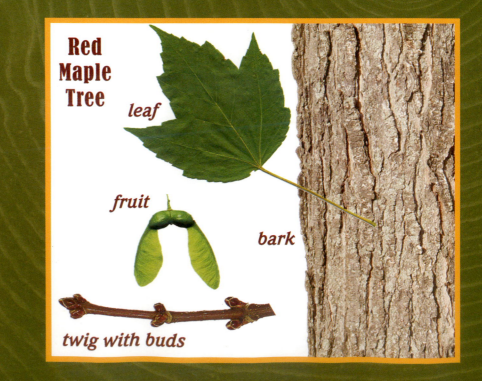

Red Maple Tree

leaf

fruit

bark

twig with buds

CHAPTER THREE

The Team

Clint McFarland and Mike Bohne became part of a massive team of scientists and foresters charged with eradicating the Asian longhorned beetle from Worcester. On paper, the task of eradication was simple: Find infested trees and cut them down. And then, just to be safe, cut down all the nearby trees that could serve as hosts for the beetle too, whether they are infested or not.

Survey crews alert Worcester residents to their presence in the neighborhood before inspecting trees for ALB (top), and after a day of teaching them how to identify signs of ALB in the wild, Clint and other members of his team pose with a group of young foresters-in-training (bottom).

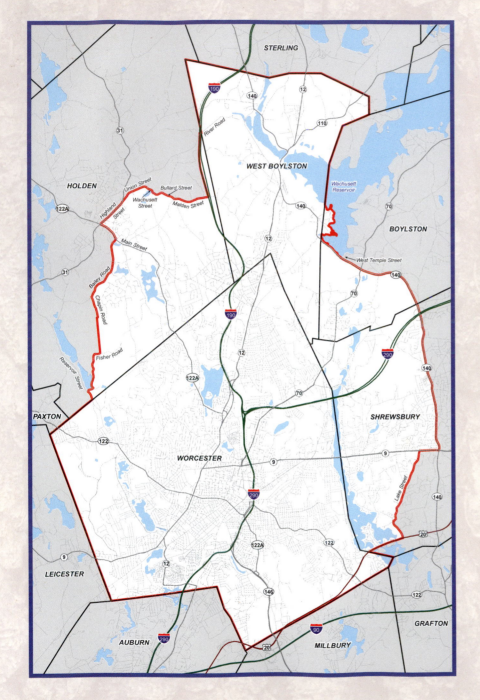

But in all the ways that count—the daily work in the forests in and around Worcester—eradication can seem impossible. Would-be beetle busters have to find infested trees in the first place, which means recognizing subtle signs of ALB presence in trees, one trunk at a time. This isn't too hard to do in city trees, but it can be overwhelming to attempt in one hundred square miles of urban and wild forest that contains *millions* of trees.

In September 2008, teams of surveyors trained in the art of identifying ALB oviposition pits, frass, and exit holes fanned out into Worcester neighborhoods to study the trees lining streets and backyards. They also spread out into the woods around the city, bushwhacking through patches of forest in search of ALB. Whenever an infested tree was identified, it was marked with bright orange paint so that crews could find it later and cut it down.

The residents of Worcester County got involved, too. Local groups organized training sessions during which the general public could learn how to spot signs of ALB for themselves. Men, women, and children

Survey crews look for signs of ALB in Worcester's urban forest.

were encouraged to monitor the trees in their backyards, neighborhoods, and schoolyards.

While professional and amateur surveyors scanned trees from the ground, a team of expert climbers was brought in to do the same thing from the air. Using ropes to scale a tree and hang in its canopy, climbers were able to examine closely the trunks and branches that were difficult or impossible to see from the ground. They looked for the now-familiar signs of ALB damage and, when found, marked the tree in question for removal.

Within two months of the discovery of ALB in Worcester, Clint's survey teams had found hundreds of adult beetles and marked thousands of infested trees for removal. They now had a small window of time during which to accomplish two massive tasks: cut down all the beetle-laden trees that had been found so far and keep looking for the ones they'd missed. They had ten months to do it; after that a new crop of adult beetles would begin to emerge from the trees.

This girl joined an ALB survey training run by the Greater Worcester Land Trust. She didn't find any beetles on this day, but she learned what to look for.

The attempt to eradicate ALB from Worcester was deemed critical to saving the northeast forest, but it was also becoming devastating for the people who lived there. Residents were giving up beloved trees, communities were losing green parks, and more than one hundred square miles of the county were placed under strict quarantine. (This meant cut wood of any kind could not be moved out of the area.) Hardest of all, perhaps, was that no one was really sure when or even if the eradication process would work. Could every single infested tree be found and removed? Could scientists and surveyors ensure that not even one beetle was overlooked?

A woman photographs ALB damage during a public training program (left). Trees found to be infested with ALB are marked with brightly colored tape (top right) or paint (bottom right).

"There are certain things that lend themselves to eradication," Clint insists.

By which he means the very long life cycle of the beetle and its poor flying skills. Until eradication is actually accomplished, though, the people of Worcester have no guarantee that the difficult eradication process will result in a beetle-free city.

If there was a bright side to this difficult situation, it was this: the infestation in Worcester provided a unique opportunity to learn about Asian longhorned beetles. Until now, most fieldwork on the beetle had been done in China, or in the limited urban forests of big cities such as New York and Chicago. In Worcester, for the first time, forest health scientists and beetle specialists could study ALB in the wild in North America. If their work helped us to better understand the beetle—perhaps even uncover a foolproof eradication method—then the deforestation of Worcester would be easier to bear.

In the photo above, crews prepare to remove all ALB host trees from Worcester's Dodge Park. The photo on the right shows the exact same view of the park after the cut.

Beetle Busting

Surveying

Joining a tree survey team in the field requires training in the art of identifying trees, especially the types known to host Asian longhorned beetles. It also requires a serious commitment to adventure. Among the hazards awaiting surveyors in the woods are poison ivy (and related rash-producing forest plants), yellowjackets (and related stinging insects), ticks (year round), glass and metal shards (surprisingly common and easy to accidentally kneel on), neighborhood dogs (who mostly don't like strangers traipsing through their woods), and, in New England at least, weather conditions ranging from frigid to frying. According to the veteran surveyor Russell Wilmot, though, these aren't even the hardest parts of the job.

"If you look at an oak long enough," Russell says, "it becomes a maple."

By which he means that identifying trees and scouring them for signs of ALB damage for six or seven hours a day can get tedious. The women and men who have taken up this task in Worcester have to keep their minds alert. They work in groups, backing up one another in the field and providing oft-needed second opinions. Surveyors are also tested regularly to make sure their tree-identification and beetle-damage-identification skills stay sharp.

The tools of this unique trade are simple enough: binoculars, a thick crayon for marking surveyed trees, a tape for measuring the diameter of those trees, a laser for directing coworkers to marks too high to point at, a knife, and a map. Depending on the time of year, surveyors also pack layers of clothing, snowshoes, bug spray, and extra water.

"We work in some miserable conditions," says Russell, "but we're outside. All day. And we love it."

A surveyor measures the diameter of a tree in Worcester's city forest.

Climbers search for Asian longhorned beetles in the trees of Worcester's Dodge Park.

32

Every tree climb begins with a visual inspection of the structure and integrity of the tree and its immediate surroundings. A climber looks for signs of physical damage or weakness. She (or he) scans the area around the base of the tree, taking note of stumps, rocks, water, animals, picnic tables—anything at all that could be a hazard to the task of getting into and out of the tree. When satisfied that the tree is safe to climb, she draws a throw ball and line from a cube-shaped pouch at her feet and casts it up into a notch between a sturdy branch and the main trunk of the tree. She uses this line to pull up a stronger rope—her primary climbing line. When the primary line is secure, the climber clips her harness to it, ties a perfect friction knot, and lifts herself into the air.

"That is the hardest part of the whole thing," says Jackie Beebe, who started climbing trees in New York City and now hunts ALB damage in the treetops of Worcester. "The initial lift feels . . . goofy. It's an awkward feeling."

Once she's made her way into the canopy, though, everything changes. "From the ground, you're seeing only fifty percent of the tree, only the bottoms of all the branches. But up there we can move around and see the whole tree. I can look head-on at other trees, at high branches, and not have to deal with the limited visibility or tough angles you are stuck with on the ground."

There are a few things you should know about being a climber. First of all, almost anyone can do it. Climbers can be tall or

short, male or female, thin or stocky, outgoing or shy, naturalists or athletes, or something else entirely. Many climbers, believe it or not, are afraid of heights.

"I don't even like ladders," says Jackie's colleague Zack Standring, "but my fear keeps me on point."

All climbers, though, particularly those working for the ALB eradication program in Massachusetts, have a commitment to their task. "We are here to stop the beetle. We believe in what we are doing," says Melissa Levangie, a world champion climber and another member of Clint's climbing crew. "I do this because I want to save the northeast forest."

Tree Removal and Replantng

Cutting down trees in the middle of a busy city—particularly old, large trees—is a complicated affair. Downing an eighty-foot tree with a massive trunk set at the edge of a major roadway *during rush hour* takes patience and skill. Sawyers (men and women professionally trained to cut trees with saws) typically remove trees in pieces, starting with the canopy and moving down to the trunk. Tremendous care is taken to protect nearby structures and roadways. In tight quarters, the tree removal crews get creative, sometimes using cranes to lift machinery into inaccessible spaces.

To be sure that all beetle larvae and pupae lurking inside an infested tree are killed, each trunk section and every branch is chipped into pieces less than an inch in every dimension. Sometimes this is done at the site of removal, and sometimes it is done at a designated chipping site.

33

In this series of images, which begins on the previous page, a trained sawyer rides a crane into the tree canopy in Worcester's Dodge Park. With the help of the crane, he removes an ALB-infested tree, starting with the crown.

Tough logistics was not the only problem for tree removal units in Worcester. No one who lived in the city wanted to see trees cut down, so emotions ran high. It takes a very long time to grow a tree big enough to provide cooling shade and a leafy view. When one of these grand old trees comes down, the landscape is changed for a lifetime. There just isn't much you can do to restore shade and leaf right away. You plant a new tree—Clint and his team have planted tens of thousands in Worcester to replace those they've cut down—but you have to wait for it to grow. In Worcester, it will take twenty or thirty years for the canopy being removed by the eradication program to grow back. (How old will *you* be in thirty years?)

CHAPTER FOUR

An ALB-infested forest known as the Delaval tract in Worcester, Massachusetts.

E arly in their work, members of Clint's survey team identified a small forest on the edge of Worcester that was infested with Asian longhorned beetles. The land was covered by a variety of large trees whose tops blended together in a tight canopy. This was not a city forest, but a true—albeit small—*wild* forest. To Mike Bohne and his fellow forest entomologists, pathologists, and botanists, this was as exciting as it was scary.

The Forest

"Here was an opportunity to study the beetle in a North American forest for the first time," Mike said. "It was unprecedented. We'd never had an opportunity to collect data like this before."

There was one problem, though: the trees in that infested forest were scheduled to be cut down. Immediately. But Clint recognized the value of studying the forest before it was cut, of learning what could be learned about the beetle. He gave Mike's team a little leeway.

"We had a week," said Mike, "and that was it. There was no other way."

So, in the middle of December, with temperatures in Worcester hovering in the teens, Mike, an entomologist named Kevin Dodds, and a team of colleagues scrambled to collect as much information as they could from this stand, or group, of trees.

"The first thing we did," says Kevin, "was go in and make circular plots throughout the stand."

These plots were big: imagine a circle drawn inside half of an NBA basketball court and you've got a good estimate of the size. Once

Mike Bohne and Kevin Dodds collect data from an infested forest stand in Worcester.

the circles were marked out on the forest floor with flags, the team stepped inside and documented every single tree. They identified the species and noted the diameter, canopy size, and whether or not the tree showed signs of ALB damage. The team collected data from hundreds of trees, large and small, in twenty different circle plots.

"This wasn't rocket science," Mike says. "It was just good old-school forestry."

Old-school forestry, it turns out, can be pretty powerful in a situation like this one. The information Mike and Kevin collected would eventually allow their team to paint an extremely accurate picture of this particular forest. Painting that picture would come later, though, back in Kevin's lab. For now, the team simply collected the data, circle after circle.

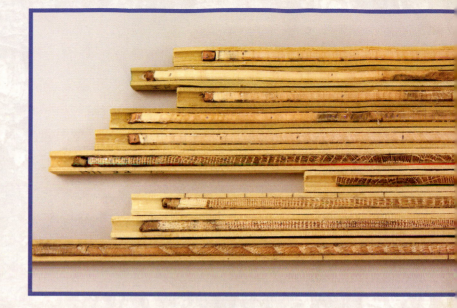

Tree cores, such as the ones Mike and Kevin collected in Worcester, are laid side by side in the lab. Because the cores are fragile, each is glued into a wooden support. Can you make out the tree rings in some of these cores?

As the week wore on, the weather in Worcester deteriorated. Forecasters first predicted rain, then warned of a cold front. The team members finished gathering their circle-plot data and began collecting other types of information about the forest.

"We wanted to look at how trees in a forest setting respond to being attacked by ALB. Do they decline rapidly? Is it a big deal to have only a couple oviposition sites or only a few exit holes in a tree?" Kevin wondered.

In other words, how much damage was ALB actually doing in North American forests? If left alone, would the beetles eventually kill trees? Could trees withstand small amounts of beetle damage?

"These were things we were hoping to tease out," says Kevin.

They collected core samples from several trees. These samples contained a small record of the life history of each tree. In the lab, after sanding, the growth rings in each core would be examined under a microscope and used to determine how individual trees in this stand grew from year to year. By comparing cores taken from trees harboring ALB with cores from trees without ALB damage, Kevin and his colleagues hoped to learn what impact the beetles had on the growth of an individual tree over time.

The team's final task in the soon-to-be-cleared forest was to examine the success rate of beetle eggs laid on various trees. This involved dissecting ALB-infested trees cookie by cookie, recording the fate of every single egg laid on a given tree's surface.

This is just as difficult as it sounds. The team's sawyer felled chosen trees one at a time. Once he had it on the ground, the sawyer cut the trunk into one-meter chunks, or bolts. Team members studied each bolt, meticulously describing every ALB oviposition site they found before cutting the bolts into smaller cookies.

"We would then dig into that attack and find out what happened. Did the beetle lay an egg? Did the egg hatch?" Kevin said.

Using pocket knives and picking tools, they tracked each larva through the tree, from its oviposition pit through the bark and into the heart of the tree. Sometimes the trail ended with a dead larva; sometimes scientists were able to track a larva all the way to its pupation chamber and beyond, to its eventual exit hole.

December 8, 2008, dawned gray and

38

wet in Worcester and, as predicted, turned very cold. By noon, all of central Massachusetts would be enveloped in an epic ice storm.

"We could see ice building up on the understory," remembers Kevin, "and by two p.m. we had to leave. It was coming down really hard and we were worried about stuff breaking."

Stuff like branches and tree trunks. Remember, the team was working in a thick forest infested with a tree pest known to chew tunnels through trees, weakening their branches and trunks. Team members wore hard hats as they worked, but at a certain point safety dictated evacuation. They took their data and headed home.

In the photos on these pages, Kevin Dodds and his colleagues core trees in the infested forest just before an ice storm moves in. The man in the foreground of the photo on the left is operating the increment borer, a hand-cranked T-shaped drill with a hollow bit. As the bit is forced into the tree, it cuts a thin stick of wood, called a tree core. (For a look at tree cores, see page 37.)

These images show Mike, Kevin, and a colleague dissecting ALB-infested trees in Worcester in the fall of 2011. Trees are downed (top left), cut into bolts (bottom left), cut into cookies (bottom center), and then dissected with picking tools (bottom right). Sometimes the team can follow an egg-laying site to the larval stage (top right) and beyond.

More Beetle Busting

In addition to Mike and Kevin's forestry team, other specialists have flocked to Worcester to study the Asian longhorned beetles there. Each team hopes to squeeze as much knowledge as possible out of a very difficult situation.

Infested bolts of wood from Worcester are kept in a secure room at the Plant Protection and Quarantine Lab in Cape Cod, Massachusetts. The beetles that emerge from this wood are studied in the laboratory.

Lab Studies

Clint's team regularly set aside pieces of infested trees and branches for researchers at the U.S. Department of Agriculture's Plant Protection and Quarantine (PPQ) Laboratory in nearby Cape Cod, Massachusetts. The scientists at this facility are raising a colony of ALB in a completely sealed lab environment— they use petri dishes, gauze strips, synthetic food, and fresh maple branches to do it—and testing their ideas about how the beetle grows and develops. They study the infested wood in order to more closely pinpoint the year the Worcester infestation began (current estimates suggest the early 1990s) and compare the DNA of Worcester's beetles with the DNA of beetles from other North American infestations to learn if and how they might be related. A steady source of beetles and infested wood from Worcester is crucial for this work.

Dr. Maya Nehme hangs a trap designed to attract ALB on a roadside tree in Worcester.

41

Trap Studies

Many insects communicate with chemicals. These chemicals are often produced in their own bodies, and some of them are involved in attracting mates. Insects have also been known to respond to chemicals produced by trees and plants. Dr. Maya Nehme, a postdoctoral student in the Entomology Department at Pennsylvania State University, spent years studying how Asian longhorned beetles communicate and interact with both beetle-produced and plant-produced chemicals. In Worcester, Dr. Nehme was able to test her theories about the exact combinations of these compounds that are most attractive to Asian longhorned beetles. She designed large traps out of cardboard and baited them with the recipe of chemical attractants she felt would attract female beetles. She then hung these traps from trees throughout Worcester county—in infested areas as well as in areas thought not to harbor beetles—in hopes that they would help locate beetles. They did.

"The beauty of the traps is that they can be surveyed all through the season," Dr. Nehme explains. "Anytime you catch a beetle, then you know you have an infestation in that area."

Thunder, a sharp-nosed beagle, has been trained to detect the smell of Asian longhorned beetle frass in and around trees.

Sniffer Dogs

Perhaps one of the most popular groups studying ALB in Worcester comes from the National Detector Dog Training Center in Georgia. Monica Errico, a training specialist, and her team of canine handlers thought their sniffer dogs, trained to catch the scent of agricultural contraband at our nation's airports and borders, could be trained to pick up the distinct scent of Asian longhorned beetles. Clint provided vials of beetle frass collected from sites in Worcester, and Monica began training her three best dogs—Thunder, Blaze, and RJ. After months of work at the center in Georgia, the dogs traveled to Worcester to practice sniffing out ALB in the field. They passed early tests easily, distinguishing between the frass of Asian longhorned beetles and the frass of related beetles.

"Our goal is to use them to detect ALB," says Monica. Results so far have been "very, very encouraging."

CHAPTER FIVE

The Data

Back in the lab, Kevin began analyzing his team's data. He started with the circle plots. These twenty sets of data contained the species, size, and ALB status of every single tree in twenty large areas of the forest being studied. Using computer modeling programs, Kevin combined the data sets, averaged them, and expanded the results so that he had, in the end, a detailed and highly accurate picture of not just the twenty large circular areas, but also the entire one-hundred-acre forest.

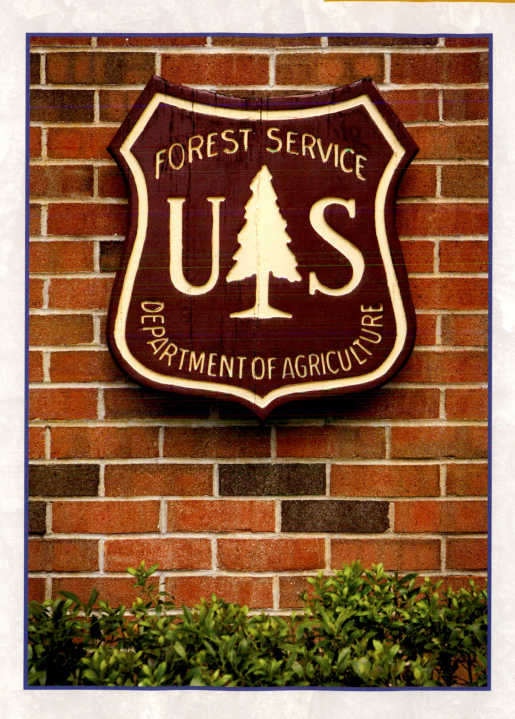

From this analysis, he learned that the forest contained fourteen tree species, several of which are known to be ALB hosts. These included red maple, sugar maple, sweet birch, white ash, and various elms. To figure out if the beetles preferred any one of these trees over the others, Kevin compared the number of infested and uninfested trees of each species that his team had recorded. The results were striking. Even though the Asian longhorned beetle is feared for its ability to survive on many different types of trees, in this patch of natural forest, it showed a clear preference for one type.

"Red maples were attacked more frequently," says Kevin.

The data also suggested that Asian longhorned beetles more readily attack larger trees.

"Based on that," Mike Bohne says, "you can make recommendations for the future. If you want to survey for ALB in a forest, look for the tallest red maple with the tallest canopy. That is where you should start."

ALB Attack on Maple Trees

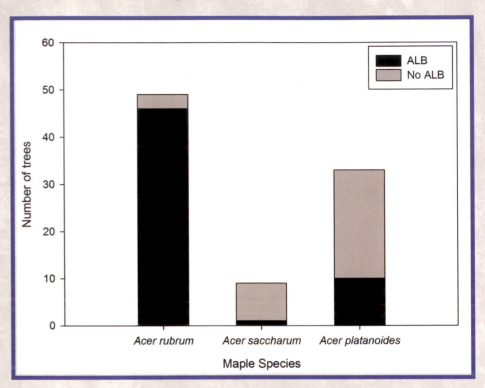

This bar graph shows the rate at which Asian longhorned beetles were found to attack red maple (*Acer rubrum*), sugar maple (*Acer saccharum*) and Norway maple (*Acer platanoides*) trees in a natural forest.

To understand how ALB affected the growth and development of individual trees in the wild, Kevin's team examined the tree cores they had collected in the forest. Each core was dried and sanded so that the individual tree rings were clearly visible under a microscope. Cores from uninfested trees were used for comparison, and in all cases the growth rings for specific years were identified. Two years proved particularly useful for this analysis: 1981 and 1953.

The growth rings for these two years were known to be unusually small in the trees of Worcester County. That's because in 1981 an outbreak of gypsy moth caterpillars had resulted in severe defoliation of local trees; every tree in the area

Tree cores and coring equipment in the lab.

grew poorly that year. Likewise, in June of 1953 a tornado ripped through Worcester and reduced the growth of surviving trees in the area. Using these pointer years to orient themselves in each tree core, Kevin and his colleagues were able to compare the growth of trees infested with ALB and trees that showed no signs of infestation. Surprisingly, the results showed that Asian longhorned beetles had little if any effect on the overall growth of the trees it infested, at least in the case of the infestation of this one small forest plot.

Kevin found something else interesting in his team's data from this parcel of natural forest in Worcester. It had to do with a theory that had been put forward by scientists studying ALB in Chicago and other places. These studies suggested that the ability of ALB to move across a landscape was limited. Further studies in laboratory and natural settings seemed to support

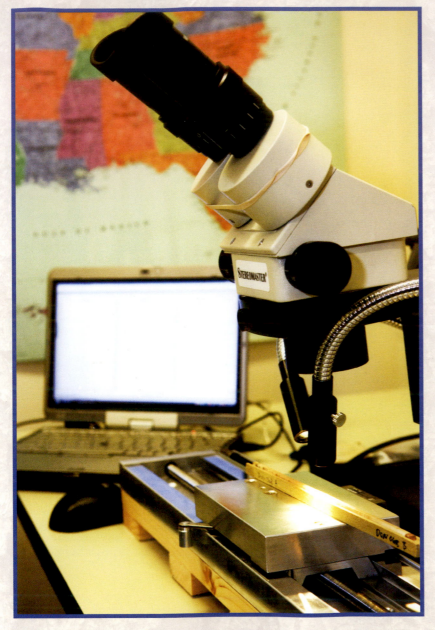

The annual growth rings of tree cores are analyzed under a microscope.

the idea that when they are given the chance to move, adult Asian longhorned beetles don't. At least not very far. In some of these studies, the beetles preferred trees located at the very edge of a forest, at the place where trees met open land. Together, these results suggested that ALB would stick to the city or, at worst, to the edges of a surrounding forest. Everyone in Worcester—and, of course, the other North American cities battling ALB infestations—hoped this was true.

"We would have liked to confirm the edge theory too," says Mike, "but the data speaks for itself."

And what their data says is this: Asian longhorned beetles don't stick to edges at all. In the forest they studied, Mike and Kevin found beetle damage spread fairly evenly throughout the stand. Asian longhorned beetles had not stopped at the edges. They'd moved right through the forest.

"We've been able to work in three stands now, characterizing ALB attacks and doing some science on what will happen if this beetle escapes into the open forest," Mike says.

And what will happen if ALB moves into the open hardwood forests of northeastern North America—forests that begin right outside Worcester, Massachusetts, and spread northward into southern Canada and westward to the Great Lakes? Kevin and Mike believe it will begin the slow but steady process of completely changing those forests.

CHAPTER SIX

The Hard Truth

C hange happens naturally in a forest. When a tree dies, for example, it topples over and opens up space. If it was a large tree, the forest floor around where it once stood is suddenly bathed in sunlight again. Seeds in the soil, reacting to this newfound energy, germinate and grow. Since there are

Ryan birding at the old landfill site.

PLANTS STAGE
FIRST 5 YEARS

SHRUB STAGE
6–25 YEARS

YOUNG FOREST
26–50 YEARS

MATURE FOREST
51–100 YEARS

This single drawing shows many decades of forest succession, starting with young plants growing up in a newly cleared area (plants stage) and ending with a forest of tall trees (mature forest).

likely to be a variety of seed types germinating at the same time, competition among them begins immediately. Over the next decade or so, a tug-of-war over soil nutrients, sunlight, and water results in near constant change as different plants, shrubs, and trees take the lead at various times. Almost certainly, in the long term, a tree will win. As it grows taller and broader, its canopy will eventually stretch high enough and wide enough to block the sun again.

The difference between this natural change and the sort of event that might be touched off by an ALB infestation is mostly scale. If ALB moves into the northeast hardwood forest and we don't attempt to stop it, the forest could undergo a massive change in composition in a relatively short time. Some of our favorite trees—trees we use to make furniture, produce syrup, and entice fall tourists—will be replaced en masse. This will affect people emotionally and financially. Just as worrisome, rapidly changing forest environments will have a deep impact on the animals that live in them.

Interestingly, though, this sort of massive change *has* happened in our forests before. For example, in the early 1900s, one out of every four trees in the northeast hardwood forest was an American chestnut. They were, by all accounts, magnificent trees, beloved for their majesty and strength. Starting in 1904, chestnut trees began to get sick and die. The cause was a fungus, one that probably entered the country on a shipment of foreign chestnut trees. Although the foreign trees were resistant to the fungus, the American trees were not. Within twenty years, an estimated three billion chestnut trees contracted the fungus, developed chestnut blight, and died. The forest survived, of course, but it no longer contained mature chestnut trees.

The disease that took down the chestnut—and an unrelated disease that took hundreds of millions of American elm trees a short time later—targeted one specific species of tree. Asian longhorned beetles, as you now know, are capable of damaging a variety of tree species. If left unchecked in the forest, would ALB eventually kill all the members of the wide variety of trees it can inhabit in the wild? Could the forest absorb all those losses at once? These questions are really hard to answer. But they drive Clint McFarland, Mike Bohne, Kevin Dodds, and their colleagues to continue their work.

Ironically, one of the places where we can gain a sense of what an unchecked ALB infestation might do to a forest is in the parts of Worcester County that were affected by eradication efforts. In tracts of wooded land that were cut down to stop the beetle, all potential ALB host trees were removed at once. This is what was done in Ryan Zumpano's woods, for example. And because he has paid close attention, Ryan can now tell us a bit about what has happened there since the cut.

Ryan and his classmates in the Biodiversity Club spend a few Saturday mornings every spring counting bird species in the forest at the old landfill. They also join Mr. Palmer each May in an annual statewide bird census called Bird-a-thon.

"At the cut site, within a two-hour walk, there were four or five different habitats," says Mr. Palmer. "So it was always a pretty great place to see a concentration of birds."

Most years, Mr. Palmer's Bird-a-thon team records fifty or so species there in just a couple of hours. It takes a full day of driving to multiple other locations in Massachusetts to log another fifty species of birds.

In May of 2011, just two months after every potential ALB host tree, infested or not, was removed from the forest, Ryan and Mr. Palmer recorded thirty-two species of birds. They noticed an increase in the number of hawks and other birds of prey. (They think these birds moved in to feast on the variety of ground animals exposed by the removal of so many trees.) Other than that, things didn't seem to have changed all that much.

The next spring, however, was different. On Bird-a-thon day, Mr. Palmer and his team counted only seven species of birds at the cut site.

Ryan's handwritten record of Bird-a-thon data for the old landfill site over the past decade. Additional data, written on the back side of this sheet, is not shown.

50

Mr. Palmer and Ryan
at the old landfill.

"It was birds you'd see in a Walmart parking lot," says Ryan. "House sparrows and things like that. The birds we went to that spot to see just weren't there. They didn't come back."

But in the spring of 2013, three years after the cut, students began to record more bird activity during their Saturday walks. At Bird-a-thon that spring, Mr. Palmer's team spotted twenty-three species. Succession—the slow and steady return of trees to an area cleared of them—has begun. And it appears that at least some of the animals that once called that forest home are returning too.

"Nature can heal itself," Mr. Palmer says. "The first year after the cut was devastating. Every year, though, there is new growth that changes the nature of the environment at that site. And so different species come in. Eventually it should go back to something like it was."

And he's right.

"But it will never be the same forest," Ryan insists.

And the thing is, he's right too.

It seems there will always be two sides— pros and cons, good news and bad news—to the ALB eradication story. There is good evidence, for example, that Clint's team is making progress in the eradication effort. In the fall of 2008, the year ALB was first discovered in Worcester, government workers collected buckets of Asian longhorned beetles. There were so many that an official number was never recorded. In 2009, after a year of intensive tree survey and removal, only 33 beetles were collected. In 2010, the number jumped to 176, but it fell back to 32 in 2011, and to 13 in 2012. As this book goes to press, 16 Asian longhorned beetles have been collected. Clint believes this trend is a sign that the eradication program is working. He predicts it will take several more years—until 2018, at least—to completely eradicate Asian longhorned beetles from Worcester County.

An aerial view of a Worcester neighborhood in which all ALB host trees were removed. To get an idea of how changed this area is, compare this image to the one on page 20, which shows a nearby neighborhood whose trees were spared.

"I wouldn't be part of this program," says Clint, "if I didn't think we could realize what we are after."

And there is more good news. Although more than 33,000 trees have been removed from the Worcester landscape since 2008, tens of thousands of new ones have been planted in their place. These trees were chosen for their resistance to Asian longhorned beetles. When they reach maturity, the treescape in Worcester will be leafy, diverse, and ALB-resistant.

"In thirty years," Mike Bohne predicts, "Worcester will have a very beautiful, probably crown jewel, urban forest."

Volunteers have helped replant thousands of trees in Worcester County, including these at Dodge Park.

More replanting at Dodge Park.

But to the people who live there, 2018 is a long way off and thirty years is an eternity. What's more, there are troubling setbacks to worry about.

In 2010, for example, two Asian longhorned beetles were found on a tree sixty miles from Worcester, in the city of Boston. After a massive investigation, Clint and his team believe this was a very small satellite infestation. That is, there is evidence that these beetles were accidentally moved from Worcester to Boston in cut firewood. The beetles emerged from the firewood, mated, found a host tree, and laid a few eggs. Six trees were removed and after extensive study were found to contain only two fresh emergence holes. Two adult beetles were captured. Further surveys in the area turned up no more beetles and no sign that their relatives might be lurking in the city forest.

In the summer of 2011, however, an Asian longhorned beetle was found in Bethel, Ohio. Bethel is as rural as Worcester and as close to natural forests, and the infestation there is believed to be large. So even if we do stop the beetle in Worcester, can we stop it in Bethel, too?

A sycamore tree in winter.

And if we stop it in Bethel, can we be sure another infestation isn't lurking in the trees of some other North American city?

In the end, the hardest part of Asian longhorned beetle infestations—in Worcester and elsewhere—may not be lost trees but, rather, this reality: eradication can be a success in one place and still fail on a grander scale. In addition to those in New York and Ohio, eradication efforts are now under way in Austria, Japan, Canada, France, Germany, Italy, England, and, most recently, Switzerland. Just as we humans stop the beetle in one location, it pops up in another.

Believe it or not, successful ALB eradication will depend heavily on people like you. (Yes, you!) Every North American ALB infestation—New York, Chicago, Jersey City, Toronto, Worcester, Boston, Bethel—was discovered by a private citizen, an observant person with no training in entomology who saw something unusual (a massive black and white beetle with blue feet and striped antennae) and did something about it (called an ALB hotline, or something like it, to report what he or she had found). If we are to keep Asian longhorned beetles out of our trees, we need to keep our eyes on those trees, watching the insects we see there and alerting officials to anything that looks remotely suspicious.

One of the many Worcester homes that lost a neighboring tree.

We humans have taken our stand in Worcester and tried, to the best of our ability, to stop the spread of one invasive beetle. (Sadly, there are enough invasive organisms causing problems for our forests to support a whole other book.) We've tried to save the forest from another round of massive change. We've done it because there is good reason to believe it might work. Whatever happens elsewhere, Clint and his team will almost certainly eradicate the Asian longhorned beetle from Massachusetts. Someday— maybe not soon, but someday—Worcester's wild and city forests will return. But the really hard questions will remain.

Was cutting those trees the right thing to do?

If cutting trees in one community today would save the trees in your backyard tomorrow, would it be worth it?

Would you feel the same way if you lived in that community and the trees being cut down were the only ones in your entire neighborhood?

A view of Worcester's leafy canopy.

Author's Note

The scientist and activist Jane Goodall once said, "Change happens by listening and then starting a dialogue with the people who are doing something you don't believe is right." On March 3, 2010, with this idea firmly in mind, I attended my first community meeting on Asian longhorned beetles. ALB

58

had just been discovered in trees in my small town in central Massachusetts. Plans were under way to remove the infested trees and, to my dismay, a whole lot of other trees, too. The issue of invasive species had come home, so to speak, and at stake were not just any old trees, but *my* trees. The sycamore I sat under as I watched my boys play Little League baseball, the maples lining the

nature trail behind the elementary school my daughter attended, the shagbark hickories on my front lawn: I thought they were all in danger. (Two of the three species were. I now know that shagbark hickories are not ALB hosts.) So I went to the meeting in order to start a conversation with the people who were going to be cutting down those trees, people who were doing something I didn't feel was right. That's where I met Clint McFarland.

In the beginning, I did not intend to write a book; I just wanted to save the trees I loved. Somewhere along the way, though, I decided to tell the ALB story. As a result, my conversation with Clint became a regular part of my working life for several years. He shared his knowledge of and passion for insects, answered my many questions, and bravely confronted this basic truth: I don't entirely agree with him on the issue of ALB eradication. Our long conversation has nonetheless been honest, pointed, well-intentioned, and respectful. I am deeply grateful to him for that.

Because of where I live, and because my friends and neighbors here are an intelligent, thoughtful, and curious bunch, the conversation spilled over into my personal life, too. I am sincerely grateful to have had each and every one of these discussions; they are a big part of this book.

Jane Goodall was right: dialogue is key. I may not be sure that ALB eradication is going to work long term, but I am sure that the men and women executing this bold and ambitious plan, the men and women searching, observing, climbing, studying, marking, cutting, and learning about my trees—our trees—are good people. They believe in what they do. And I believe in them.

To Learn More

Read

Sniffer Dogs: How Dogs (and Their Noses) Save the World by Nancy Castaldo (Boston: Houghton Mifflin Harcourt, 2014).

Science Warriors: The Battle Against Invasive Species by Sneed Collard III (Boston: Houghton Mifflin, 2008).

Kaufman Field Guide to Insects of North America by Eric R. Eaton and Kenn Kaufman (New York: Houghton Mifflin, 2007).

The Sibley Guide to Trees by David Allen Sibley (New York: Knopf, 2009).

Watch

Bugged: The Race to Eradicate the Asian Longhorned Beetle

Find out more at www.buggeddocumentary.com.

Lurking in the Trees

Find out more at www.dontmovefirewood.org/documentaries.html.

Explore

U.S. Department of Agriculture ALB website
www.aphis.usda.gov/plant_health/plant_pest_info/asian_lhb/index.shtml

Massachusetts Asian Longhorned Beetle Cooperative Eradication Program website
massnrc.org/pests/alb

Beetle Busters, an outreach curriculum from the USDA
www.AsianLonghornedBeetle.com.
(Please note that although this curriculum and the book you are reading share a title and explore the same topic, they are not affiliated in any way.)

Get involved with the hunt for Asian longhorned beetles
asianlonghornedbeetle.com/get-involved/alb-hunt

***i*MapInvasives**
www.imapinvasives.org

Center for Invasive Species and Ecosystem Health
www.bugwood.org

The Science of Tree Rings, a presentation from the Department of Geography, University of Tennessee
web.utk.edu/~grissino

Glossary

bolt
A cut segment of a tree trunk or branch.

botanist
A scientist who studies plants, trees, and other members of the plant kingdom.

canopy
The uppermost layer of a forest, consisting mostly of the branches and leaves atop resident trees.

cookie
The flat and round disk of wood obtained by cutting a tree trunk or branch in cross section.

dendrochronology
The study of growth rings and the history of individual trees; scientists who do this work are called dendrochronologists.

entomologist
A scientist who studies insects.

eradication
The active removal of all living members of a particular species from a particular place.

forest
An environment characterized by a collection of plants, bushes, trees, and the animals that live in and around them. Natural (or wild) forests are large tracts of land that have not been altered or developed by humans. City (or urban) forests grow amid areas of human development.

forestry
The study of forest environments and their management.

frass
Insect poop.

growth ring
One of the faint rings of woody tissue visible inside the trunk and limbs of trees that represent the tree's annual growth in diameter.

grub
The larval stage of a beetle.

heartwood
The wood in the center of a tree trunk or branch.

host tree
In this book, the term refers to any tree that can support the life cycle of the Asian longhorned beetle.

larva (larvae)
The part of the beetle life cycle that comes after the egg; more than one larva are called larvae.

oviposition site
A scratched-out site on the bark of a host tree where an adult female Asian longhorned beetle lays her egg.

pathologist
A scientist who studies diseases, how they start, and how they develop over time.

pupation chamber
A hollow place deep inside a tree, chewed out by a larval Asian longhorned beetle, which serves as a resting place as the beetle changes to its adult form.

sawyer
A person skilled in the art of cutting trees.

species
The most basic category of organism classification; members of the same species look the same and can reproduce.

springwood
Wood produced by trees during the spring and characterized by large cells with very thin walls; springwood forms a light-colored ring that can be seen when a tree or branch is cut in cross section.

stand
A group of trees growing near one another.

summerwood
Wood produced by trees during the summer and characterized by small cells with thick walls; summerwood forms a dark-colored ring that can be seen when a tree or branch is cut in cross section.

tree core
A thin stick of wood—usually extending from the bark to the center of a trunk—that is extracted from a tree in order to study its growth rings.

vascular cambium
A special layer of tree tissue, located between the bark and the inner wood of a trunk or branch, which is responsible for producing new cells as the tree grows.

volatiles
Small quantities of chemicals that leaves release into the air and that some species of trees may use to warn each other about insect attacks.

Bibliography

This book is based primarily on personal interviews the author conducted between March 2010 and August 2013. Of the many books and scholarly articles consulted for additional research, the following were particularly valuable:

Burdick, Alan. *Out of Eden*. New York: Farrar, Straus and Giroux, 2005.

Capon, Brian. *Botany for Gardeners*. Portland: Timber Press, 2010.

Davis, Mark, et al. "Don't Judge Species on Their Origins." *Nature* 474, no. 7350 (June 9, 2011): 153.

Dodds, Kevin, and David Orwig. "An Invasive Urban Forest Pest Invades Natural Environments—Asian Longhorned Beetle in Northeastern US Hardwood Forests." *Canadian Journal of Forest Research* 41 (2011): 1729.

Elton, Charles. *The Ecology of Invasions by Animals and Plants*. Chicago: University of Chicago Press, 1958.

Haack, Robert, et al. "Managing Invasive Populations of Asian Longhorned Beetle and Citrus Longhorned Beetle: A Worldwide Perspective." *Annual Review of Entomology* 55, no. 521 (2010): 521.

Heinrich, Bernd. *The Trees in My Forest*. New York: Ecco, 1997.

Mann, Charles. *1493: Uncovering the New World Columbus Created*. New York: Vintage, 2011.

Simberloff, Daniel, et al. "Impacts of Biological Invasions." *Trends in Ecology & Evolution* 28, no. 1 (January 2013): 58.

Acknowledgments

I would like to thank the following people for their kindness and generosity during the creation of this book: Clint McFarland, Mike Bohne, Kevin Dodds, Garret DuBois, Peggy Middaugh, Ruth Seward, Quiava Brown and his Young Adult Foresters team, Monica Errico, Joe Chopko, Colin Novick, Phil Lewis, Bill Panagakos, Jodi Rymer, the students of Thorndyke Road School, Scott Knapp, Maya Nehme, Bruce Palmer, Ryan Zumpano, and the entire ALB eradication team in Worcester, Massachusetts. I'd like to send special thanks to Amy Stauffer for her patient instruction in tree identification, for her early thoughts on the manuscript, and for her friendship. Last but not least, I'd like to thank Kate Messner, Linda Urban, and Erica Zappy: you are reading these words because these three marvelous women knew what to say whenever I lost my way.

Index

Research Update

For the Asian longhorned beetle eradication effort in Worcester County to be declared a success, the number of adult beetles found in the area must be *zero* for five years in a row. In 2012, the last full year of data before this book went to press, researchers found 13 beetles in the wild. (See page 52.) The next year, they found 16 adult beetles, the year after that they found 5, and the year after that, just 1. In 2016, for the first time since the infestation was discovered, not a single adult Asian longhorned beetle was reported in the wilds of Worcester County. *Zero.* I'm typing this update in September 2017, and as of today no adult beetles have been recorded this season either. We're not there yet, but we're inching closer to eradication.

Loree Griffin Burns completed her doctoral studies in biochemistry at the University of Massachusetts Medical School. Her other Scientists in the Field books include *Life on Surtsey: Iceland's Upstart Island, Tracking Trash: Flotsam, Jetsam, and the Science of Ocean Motion,* and *The Hive Detectives: Chronicle of a Honey Bee Catastrophe,* the latter also featuring photography by Ellen Harasimowicz. Dr. Burns lives in Massachusetts with her husband and three children, smack in the middle of the Asian longhorned beetle quarantine zone. Although she befriended a few lab-raised beetles while researching this book, she hopes never to see one in the wild. LoreeBurns.com

Ellen Harasimowicz saw an Asian longhorned beetle emerge from a tree (the one on page 12) while photographing tree climbers. She had just seconds to photograph the beetle before it was captured. She lives in central Massachusetts and photographs all over the world. EllenHarasimowicz.com